Once You Had Hands

ONCE YOU HAD HANDS

POEMS

TASHA GOLDEN
photographs by Michael Wilson

HUMANIST PRESS
WASHINGTON, DC

© 2015 Tasha Golden

Humanist Press
1777 T Street NW
Washington, DC, 20009
(202) 238-9088
www.humanistpress.com

All rights reserved. No part of this book may be reproduced in whole or in part without written permission from the publisher, except in the case of brief quotations embodied in critical articles and reviews; nor may any part of this book be reprinted or reproduced or utilized in any form or by any electronic, mechanical, or other means, now known or hereafter invented, including photocopying and recording, or in any information storage or retrieval system, without written permission from Humanist Press, LLC.

Printed book ISBN: 978-0-931779-58-9
Ebook ISBN: 978-0-931779-62-6

All poems by Tasha Golden
www.tashagolden.com

Cover Photo, Author Photo, All Photographs by Michael Wilson
www.michaelwilsonphotographer.com

Cover Design by Paul Mazzoleni
www.paulmazzoleni.com

for the girls.

Italicized poems throughout
are the result of manipulating texts
by 17th century poet Henry Vaughan.

Praise for *Once You Had Hands*

"Tasha Golden's *Once You Had Hands* is a smart and moving book of poetry. There is a fierce voice here that can make you feel danger without always naming it, and it is indeed a dangerous world that we meet here. Golden has sharp senses and wit in depicting her disappointment and fury at religious promises. There is joy here too, hard won, and quietly compelling."

— **Jennifer Michael Hecht**, author of *Who Said* and *Doubt: A History*

"When 'Christian' attitudes, rituals, and abuses (physical and mental) are part of one's formative experience of the richness of life itself, how does one extricate oneself from the perversion of this 'religion' yet affirm the glory and terror of existence? This book is a feral cry that invents the only form that can contain it; it's a cry embodied in and ennobled by art, which doesn't dilute but enhances its power. I am at a loss to describe, even from the outside, that power. I can only urge you to read it."

— **James Cummins**, author of *Still Some Cake*

"Wise, desperately sad, Tasha Golden's poetry finds a sinewy resilience in rhythm. Heartbeat-like, propulsive, the beat intensifies a disturbing atmosphere in which pain and harm are perversely sexualized and aestheticized. Golden's perversions turn out to be the reverse of self-indulgence. They are an ethic and a strategy she wields against the gray meaninglessness of the problem of evil. Domestic horrors are twisted into gorgeous sequined structures that in their artifice, their passionate madness, remind us that purposeful transformation is possible."

— **Catherine Wagner**, author of *Nervous Device*

"Tasha Golden, 'ankle deep in Jeremiah,' has drunk deeply of 'God the Creator of Things that Don't Last,' a God Who broods over rural Tennessee and makes its people His own. Golden is His anti-prophet, unacknowledged female emanation of a patriarchal deity Who has despoiled too many generations of Southern women. Yet this furious book is also a work of graceful beauty. Interspersed with inspired manipulations of poems by the metaphysical Henry Vaughan, and the evocative photos of Michael Wilson, Golden's work will stay with the reader for a long time."

— **Norman Finkelstein**, author of *Track*; Professor of English, Xavier University

"One has the feeling that this clear-eyed writer set out to wield poems like glowing lanterns against a tide of darkness and loss, and finding she could not stem the tide, chose instead to illuminate the questions we are all too often afraid to ask. Turns out a writer with a nimble mind and enough courage can make the fearsome questions beautiful."

— **Linford Detweiler**, *Over the Rhine*

TABLE OF CONTENTS

Happy those early days!   1

    After You've Gone   2
    I Wanted to Be Wise   3
    When the Spirit Came   5
    They say when you speak it sounds like the thin reeds of an organ.   6
    The First Curve on the Straight and Narrow   7
    (Untitled)   8
    Push   9
    What I Won't Say to Her Face   11
    I Was Thinking of Origins   13
    No, Thank You.   14
    You Looked Over Your Shoulder Once   15
    Circle Me   17
    God the Creator of Things that Don't Last   18

That empty house   21

    Covenant   22
    The blood of would-be saints   23
    That Face   25
    ends   26
    The dream of deletion   28
    the girls   30
    We May Be at the Edge of Hope Here.   32
    An eye once pressed the thin skin on the back of a hand   33
    When they told me he was knocking   34
    (Departure)   37

Tyrant   39

    Jesus the Infertile   40
    They Talk Amongst Themselves   42
    We Shouted   43
    A Folk Song for Politicking   44

Vespers	45
Men and Brethren, What Shall We Do?	46
Of Breasts and Tennessee	48
Revelation	51
Ash and Leonard Cohen	52

the Old Silence — 55

For As Wide As This Table Is	57
The Zero	59
(For Our Struggle Is Not Against Flesh and Blood)	60
When We Left the Homestead	62
Moments Before	63
I Loved Someone Once	65

I Knew It Would Be Thus — 67

He Said He Was Dostoevsky.	68
Morphine	69
Worm	70
Things We Don't Know	73
Moses Prepares A Eulogy	74
Should This Reach You Feeling Rejected and Forlorn	75
How the Secret Got Out	76
Palm Sunday	78
Bush	79
Once You Had Hands	81

I hug a strong despair — 83

Index of Photographs — 85
About the Author — 87

Happy those early days!

Before I understood

Before the

*   altars fell,*
Fires smoking
And all that sacred pomp, and shell
Of things did fly

(Thy promises but empty words)

Almighty Love! where art thou now?

*   those once sacred mansions*
Mere emptiness and show

*   a heap of rust*

*   at best*
A pleasing story

After You've Gone

We click the latch at home
and there is silence, and a window.
It's dark. Out between the branches
streetlights. Yellow stars. And inside
the refrigerator snaps into a hum:
consecrated, dutiful, three minutes
then a break. So that the absence of it
gnaws at our ears. They weep for sound.
In the window, headlights arcing. Swept
again out of the frame. Of no use
anymore to us – those lights, that arc.
And inside there's a shifting: muscle
lifting bone. A creaking from the shoulder
nearly mute, and shuffled cotton.
The hum again, the window, yellow
stars. The branches blacken
and it's later, and the door is still
shut fast. The table's blank --
an invitation. Nothing is set down.
There's a film on our clothes, our skin,
our eyes adjusting to the dark. We hold
our things, scared if we set them down
we'll lose the last of you. We dare not brush
ourselves off; dare not brush against each other.
Yellow flickers as the trees move.
They make shadows. Now the hum
is gone again. We've all been swallowing.
We're swallowing and listening.
No one turns on the light.

I Wanted to Be Wise

If I crossed myself it was to say
there may be factors none of us
considered, being ridden
by the steam and gust of purposes
we outlined in our books.
See Figure 1:1, *Escalation of Becoming*.
Dials turn and buttons press, the same
mechanics, gentle, lithe by now
they summon priests and prophets
thick and gummed up,
smeared across the silk black throats
of radios.

And turnstiles clicking,
flesh and metal, shadow clanking,
one might think to sing oneself
through veins as deep and hidden
as a devil's lurching bowels.
Instead I crossed myself, or didn't
walk so bravely in my skin, ringed
by a band a little girl could wear,
a plain black ribbon in her hair,
all factors none of us considered –
soup bowls, paper, bottles
empty, filled in as we go.

When the Spirit Came

God, it was a howling
like a sucking down
the ancient throat, a clanging
through the sockets
where your eyes should be.

And then I felt it
in the walls –
a thousand silverfish
directionless, their crawl
a savage scurrying
behind the plaster.

I knew all the words
to make them stop,
to dry them up
so that they'd flake
into a dustheap blown
about by nervous coughs.

But I couldn't let me say them
with that still small voice
that told me
when to speak
and when to listen,
when to stutter, when to lie

and when to scratch
the walls at night to say hello
and how to know
if someone answered, how
to tell myself, *he will,
he will, he will.*

**They say when you speak it sounds
like the thin reeds of an organ.**

That when you hummed in the howls
of the deep, you prophesied, saying,
"Yea, will I enclose my voice
in pressed wood and pearl, in long-
fingered pedals beset by human feet."
Yes, Lord.
And thus have we heard your pealing
sigh, your fluted syllabic hand
as it swept our bruised carpets,
our burnished pews; as it slid,
gloved and scaled, over our grey
and wicked skins.
And thus have we swung in the dust
and luster—our Amen to your bleating
call—while beneath our feet the world
rumbles, awash in holy bass.

The First Curve on the Straight and Narrow

Her eyes shook, blue and bobbing; they made contact
with the body, hair, the nakedness of arm and leg,
the hands up by the ears. Her eyes shook; she was steady.
She held the belt, remembered how the Lord said
there would be no sin nor sorrow. But this body
at her feet was her redemption: its tears washed
every hand that'd felt her breasts
and every slap across a man's face she'd withheld
in fear and trembling; how she'd lifted up her dress
instead and begged her God for vengeance.
And this was it: this body she'd once pushed
between her legs. In thirteen years, its flesh
had swelled up feminine and dark –
it was a photograph, a mirror.
So she swung from left to right across her torso
to her mark, and the thing she shouted at it now was,
Cry, for godsakes, cry! She clenched her teeth
and swung again—*Cry!*—at the waggling ribs,
the knees drawn up, the face she couldn't see. She swung
until she felt her armpits dampen, felt saliva in her cheeks;
until she felt her breath come smoother
with each heaving on the floor. Then softly,
You can come out when you're done.
She closed the door.

(Untitled)

the wood will wait
and the coffee
take your time
it's urgent
the last report
legitimates
your grunting
for a prayer you scrape
collecting it
beneath your nails
and still
a quiet so wide
it dries your mouth
and mine

Push

We couldn't have known
these would be the children we'd bear:
these years with their sharp teeth,
their poison tails that left us
crouching and nervous, love, *nervous*,
I on the kitchen floor like an old prayer,
You wide and bright
as always, painfully hurtable. Jesus,
how I sputtered those daggers at your sweet heart
coughing the words up and into that dark Winter.
We wept; you said, "These are labor pains.
Something happens next." I nodded,
steeled and stricken.
"Push."

What I Won't Say to Her Face

o god
I'm sorry
I'm sorry
I'm sorry
o god
I'm sorry
we didn't know
we didn't know
o god
surely we'd have said something
something, anything
or bitten through our lips with fear
we didn't know
o god
the monster in the house
on the phone
under the bed
we didn't know
o god
the demon at the kitchen sink
its hand soft on our backs
we didn't know
we didn't know
o god
I'm sorry
It's too late now and it won't matter
I'm sorry
I'm so sorry
I would have slipped you something
paper, sugar, aloe
I'd have whispered to you, hidden you
in blankets at my feet

o god
once, your cheek against my cheek
I shrank away like you weren't clean
like you had bitten me
o god
our little sacrificial lamb
against the wall, the carpet, door
against the kitchen chairs, the window
how you howled

I Was Thinking of Origins

Natives, whiskey, gentlemen
Little girls, loveless unions
Tubercled lungs, rotted livers
Gone, their skin lain
Sagging, sprouting weeds
Ashen, wormed into rich earth

Of how I learned to pray
From ghost mouths, coffee
Burning, cakes and paper
Torn and browning, bleeding ink
And urgency, those souls uncertain
Yawning, crowding as if I could speak
For them, as if I could speak

No, Thank You.
*"You may keep your gifts for yourself
and give your rewards to someone else." (Daniel 5:17)*

The gift is, after all, none
but the terror that was taught me:
an Excess swallowing
the Byss and the Abyss.

You Looked Over Your Shoulder Once

Having heard some groping gesture,
some thin scratch, a meager plea,
You heaved your chest,
a cosmic fulmination in your lungs –
Then let it spill, all hot and damp
across the back of that dim planet,
as it crouched and groaned and spun and drenched,
and lived, and lived, and lived.

And the yellow of that sigh
bestained the mountains and the waters,
every nail and bone and brow;
it skimmed the skin and tips of teeth,
and soaked up bleeding into speech
all hoarse and warm on swollen tongues.
It spoke you, coughing, into being
for Creation—saying slow:

> *Here breathed one wise and good,*
> *he, God, who never did a thing but that*
> *it shone and throbbed and heaved on forward,*
> *into blind forever. Yes—*
> *Here sighed one, vast and sure,*
> *who set you quaking, looked back once*
> *(He heard a scratch)*
> *and sighed, and shrugged,*
> *and cleared his mighty throat.*
>
> *But* not to *answer,* not *addressing;*
> *not to honor groans with* Stooping—
> *But to sweep his windy table*
> *with a twinkle in his eye;*

to ready every speck and sliver,
some new Garden, Atom, Seed;
to slough his skin, anew with breath,
for yet another tender, gruesome,
bloody heartbreak of a world
for which he shall not shed a tear.

O God,

You've thus made countless worlds
and clapped your hands
and wiped them clean
But, no less lonely for these toys,
and no less bored for all your play,
and the more arrogant and cruel
for how you watch us not at all --
even for sport or Job-like gamble!
Holy cruelty we could bear -- O God,

You pierce us with your quiet,
raze the temples of our throats,
and we (our limbs outspreading) grope
and grind and curse you and your world -
for how it quivers, mute and cloying;
how it boils in your breath;
for every mark it bears that tells us only,
One was here—and Left—

Circle Me,

and as you do your feet
may etch a line our nervous fingers can touch
and photograph: the incarnate division between us,
the speakable, tastable distinction;
the scuffed scrubbed cyclops of which I am
the dilating pupil and you the ringing,
blinking edge, ever arcing, combing, tearing—
a saline whisper I won't hear.

One thing in two parts is not one thing
but two; blood and chlorine; not one, *two*,
I in the middle, and you
circling, blinking, tearing;
I the dark and dilating,
you the disappearing.

God the Creator of Things that Don't Last
"the world is passing away, and also its lusts"
(1 John 2:17)

God the etching and erasing
God the beckoning
God come lately
God the rotting wood and paper
God the sopping matches
God the lover and the leaver
God the shoulders and the back
God the wine turned back to water
God the ebbing
God the vowing
God the light always receding
God the wall the floor enclosing
God the first cause and donation
God the marriage
God the warm milk
God the circus
God the tongue
God the forehead and the temple
God the stairwell
God the welcome
God the ocean dry as hell

That empty house

                      oft have I pressed
Heaven

    not with tears alone,

But with the blood of all my soul

And yet

No voice, no   vision

    no Royal Rescue

                            only

  blackness

grief and absence

A little dust
A heap of ashes

Covenant

I will leave a remnant;
Not all the blood will drown.
Women will swallow it whole,
will spit it up into fallen little angels

They'll mop the entryways,
scrub mud from sleeves and pants
and pull them, dripping, to their breasts,
will hang them out like sails

They'll press a watery earth to one cheek,
then another, chase roaches from the table,
hoard boxes of wet grass for kissing
late at night

when all the blistered hands are still
and all the lips are dry and parted;
when the wine becomes a stain
in the last corner of each glass

the blood of would-be saints

inflames my nail beds, tongue
leaks triumphant onto maps
and scripture, glazing

preservation, incantation
there are devils in it
devils

if not, explain
the bellows, whiskey, women
in the shape of moons and children

why none of them will dance
how pleasure tastes
of fear or residue of ash

why their skins grow whiter, thicker
leave no space between their legs
absorbing any telltale

flutter of a pulse

That Face
"our fear
does not have the face of a dead man
the dead are gentle to us" (Zbigniew Herbert)

I've seen him in bad drawings:
bearded, with his arms out
to the children, maybe loaded
down with bread, or (more famous)
strung out wide, his ribs a sprawling mound
between them: stacked up, sweaty bones.

I've seen him in a nightshirt,
with his owl's eyes, rolling back
a stone each night and haunting
streets and temples, with his wounds
still open; I've seen him hold the skin
closed as he walks.

And I've seen him on my ceiling
in the dark, and in the pale face
of my mother, his tongue inside her
mouth to shape the words he needs
to say: *Mercy was my milk.*
The gorging earth, that bloated calf,
suckled me dry with teeth that tore
like nails. Someday
I'll pull them one by one.

ends

ankle deep in Jeremiah,
our hips swung into John, you note

love won't erase a story
only name it something else, only

paint it over, a gloss against the lips
a bending of the light

after all
you say

the curse is hardy, jagged, licking
at the tips of buried roots, so that

our swinging-out is haunted; branches
far-flung into sky

are mere memorials to the earth
their veins a bloodline to that water

to its prickling at our feet
its seductive edge of pain

so, you say, love's no Reversal; just
the mercy of extension; just

the end that makes a story -- end
that justifies the means; that pulls

the circle from its center, so it slips

from its own name, so when it shudders

it can say it felt a bird,
a wind,
                    a grace

The dream of deletion

requires having-been
exposure
panicked looming
or at least its shadow
blooming thick
into a fixed regret.
Like the sucking
in of air after a word
as if to pull it back
the mind recoiling
draws itself
a dream in which
we're blessedly
rewound.

At some point,
even hatred
misremembers
what it is:
having fashioned itself
threading ties
umbilical
between opposing poles
until reluctant need
is lust, until
they see themselves
as one; two ends
drawn in and singing
songs that sound
for all the world
like love.

the girls

their lips were blooming, purple
tongues and specks along their cheeks
and on their narrow shoulders, propped
on stacks of ribs and tiny breasts. they smelled
of cherries and detergent, smoothed
their skirts over their knees.

but when it came to bibles,
deacons, pews,
apostles, priests, oh god

the girls were flesh and curve
all woman, eagerness and fever,
fingers dextrous, mouths lit up
in practiced ovals; when it came
to altars, parables, to shame and ash
the girls knew what to do with them—
with thick and throbbing despotism—
curtsy, psalm, and penitent admission
of their sins.

the girls were solemn: shy contrition,
tender on their tongues, wore out
their jaws and knees imagining
their bodies bawdy, hot
unholy wolves in cotton rags.
the girls, so they were told,
each had a gaping god-shaped hole
that god would fill if they believed,
he'd make them pure—body and soul.   and so

the girls lay white and wide awake
at night, a damp uncertain ache
their thighs clamped trembling shut, afraid
he might just come, or not, afraid
he'd rise engorged from ancient graves
and find his foolish virgins, shake
and climb their bones and branches, break
his silence with a kiss.

but it would never come to this.
that god, that hole, did not exist.

We May Be at the Edge of Hope Here.

I won't lie to you. When I look at your face
it's like looking at your photograph:
that bleakness in your bones, your eyes
rimmed red, your hands both coarse and frozen.
Someone behind you laughing.
But none of that is real, because your face
is just your face. It's not a photograph. You blink,
your hands move like thin fish.

So settle down. We have a light, and rosaries, and words
our mouths still fit around. We have a comb
and bread and water, lipstick and two voices
like a howling. Or a river. We aren't quiet.
We won't blow into the well and hope to hear
our breath hit water. We're soaked already, bruised,
we've grown too brazen for surrender.
Settle down; we're going under.
Open your mouth.

An eye once pressed the thin skin on the back of a hand

to see the swift   flick
   of a wing
       shadow
               diving,   lost
to sinew, bone and blood, or taste
       its foam and flutter,   quick
     spun and splintered   at the tip
         of the tongue, or
      watch it peel the thin skin
                     back
baring the wide world,   wracked
   with laughter,
            god
              curled
                   like a
                fetus
   round its throat.

But instead there was a film and flex
of husk and hair in sputters,
bruised illusion
taunting eye and lid (which, blinking,
spat their lashes
doubled back
and licked their wounds)—
an irrevocable contention
twixt the Notion and the Thing.
A sign of endings: hands will have no mercy,
leave no signs; and eyes will see
them, cheap and fallen, dirt and muscle,
liars, brutes.

When they told me he was knocking

I. This is what I thought would happen:

I would open wide the door, and God would rush in
eager, panting, like the burning lover painted
in the Song of Songs. And he would say,
Beloved! Daughter! He'd build for me a sunset
and then damn my enemies

(of which I had but one, Jill,
whose cheeks were always pink
and who had breasts
when she was ten,
and who had hips
that swayed and boys
who passed her notes
and walked her home).

So over dinner God and I would talk
about Jill's sins until we'd finished
all the ham and green beans,
leaned back in our chairs. And then God
would say, "I think we should retire
to the den. We'll stay up late tonight
and have hot tea and buttered toast."

II. This is what happened:

That night, in the quiet, with all my sisters
in their beds (and Jill too, somewhere
soft and pink and pretty in her sleep),
I felt God cough and say
he wouldn't stay up late with me

for prayer or conversation or for tea
and buttered toast. He didn't say
"I'm sorry." Instead,

he burned and bleached the mess I'd made,
hacked and carved himself the space
I hadn't left him (being small, but also
having loved a boy or two; and having wished
for breasts like Jill's; and having kept
my tithe back, greedy; having felt
between my legs).

God scoured, yes, Amen, until I wanted nothing
pretty, nothing pink, until I learned to mock
the swaying hips, refused to pierce my ears,
until I stopped my breathless wandering
in the woods behind the house
until I ate, and read devotionals
and ate, and went to church meetings
and ate, until I'd built that lover
one hell of a house

(Departure)

Climb on, brats!
We're headed for the giggling flashbulb of the moon,
for high-heeled nights in paperback.
Put down your pencils, eyes up, let me see you: yes,
the grand dilation of each pupil, ringed
by irises and nods. Climb on! all you
incorrigibles, lambs, dyed all
the color of old bone; we'll leave this and you'll wash
yourselves in dark and glaze of stars. Climb on,
you brats of mouth and hair! We're bound
to wind up somewhere. Speak up! All
together, now, your catechism –

> *holy are the paths of least resistance*
> *holy are the wheels that wear them down*
> *holy are the numbers rising*
> *holy are the chairmen of the board*

Alley oop!
We're bound, goodbye! Wave
to the clingers-on in cotton, to the smoke.
And every hand on every heart, yes,
for the glory of the engine, for the glory
of the moving, yes! for going now
with fingers round the cables, holding on.
Hold! Hold on! you pink and bony
twinings, taut, translucent
in the dusk; we'll be there soon. You'll see
the first and last, the meek nod of the giant
close of everything, while at your side, the belly
full, the crusts of bread, the stars

Tyrant

*Come see your dissolution, and weigh
What a loathed nothing you shall be one day*

    a large epistle stuffed with idle fear,
Vain dreams, and jealousies

      filled with Roman ghosts

A threadbare, goldless genealogy

Jesus the Infertile

Lord, if you'd show me
the rod in your left hand
the sword in your right,
your legs lit and manned
like the gate of the sun
the gate of the moon
If you'd cry, *enter, enter!*,
let anyone in,
if prayers were anything
but moths circling
our own dim lights

Then I could tell the barren
and the maidens, and the men
whose bellies echo with the absence
of the blood and body; tell the girls
who've only felt you moving
like a serpent, felt your spirit
like a speculum in the purple
of their skirts

I could tell them something
may yet quiver up behind the heavens
tell them their groping
in forgotten passageways may yet yield
a king

They Talk Amongst Themselves
"And God said, Let us make man in our image, after our likeness…" (Genesis 1:26)

And soon, *ex nihilo* and smoke,
they're molding skin in damp flaps
over raw meat and bone.

They pierce the seal of the lips
like foil; the air sweeps in
and rattles.

Listen! they say. Watch
the tongue squirm in there
like a serpent!

They lean in;
its first words gargle up
from slick red earth:

I know you're there, Elohim.
They laugh.
It's bluffing, bluffing.

We Shouted

in our cars over the radio
and wind; and in our churches,
call, response; and sometimes
in the parking lots of stores
and libraries. Also, cold in our garages,
while inside our TVs blared
and someone laughed; and in our dreams
where no one heard us, though we wrung sound
from our skins. And in our bathrooms
when the kids were gone, the faucets
running cold. And in our prayers, in which –
our hands in fists—our nails sliced clean
into our palms. We shouted at that flesh
as it curled: delicate and deaf.

A Folk Song for Politicking

Two ships went to war and three
will come home, three will build
the summer home for bald indulgence,
three will pitch a tent for kings,
will finger sacred texts.
Body in and body out, they'll say,
the flesh yields what it will.

Two ships went to war and three
will come home, three will parse
the stiff bones of their countrymen,
will curl their lips and make them sing.
It's how the head drops back,
they'll harmonize, *that made us
bite our tongues.*

Two ships went to war and three
will come home, three will pour
the drinks and come in sheets
and sand and wash their hands
behind the altar. Three will say,
It's what we did before, will dim
the lights and close the door.

Vespers

When you've grown
accustomed to the slapping
right hand of God Almighty, it's unnerving
to look out the window:
sunset, a luminous old car, and chain link
lying at the bottom of themselves
to the sound of The Magnetic Fields.

In such times you locate evil where you can:
insert it into cereal bowls
or carpet stains, imagine
it's the water
down your back, hot in the shower
try to hate your legs or breasts
or how your wet hair feels entangled.

But it's shit. No good fantasizing
hells to jank the smooth curve
of the earth
as it keeps launching itself
out over the foretaste and the aftermath
of How It Is.
There is only this

irrevocable lurch, the bind of skin
to mathematic probability,
death addiction birth glass sleeves stars
all blind against the window,
"The Book of Love" on repeat
like a vespers hymn,
like oil.

Men and Brethren, What Shall We Do?

Start with a sin,
                    a heartbreak; start
with skin and fire, wine
                          and water, take off
these clothes and dip
                the body
                                        slow,
      curved,
salt and vein,
                shadow, hair,
a baptistry, alchemy,
eyes closed,   head   back --

Light the corners, altars,
                          cheeks and wrists,
a blush, a nail,
                rust and blood,
a nod of the head
                    toward some holy place,
a panting breath
                        toward a hush, a pledge,
an arc of the back
                  toward the thrust,
the thrust, a prayer,
                  a swallowing
of blood and bread,
                a shudder, singing
glory, gulping *glory,*
                all that water
in your hair—

Of Breasts and Tennessee

I
of southern bodies mating,
wrung, prolific, populating
every hill, passing a spoon
from mouth to mouth and children
lined up on the gravel,
stacked in narrow plywood beds.

Maybe the moon was out,
its milk and water spilled
across the roof, and maybe
crickets sang so no one heard
the creaking of the wood,
the grisly sound of bearing fruit.

Whiskey, dirt, and Tennessee-
-bred progenies, his knees
astride her hips, his breath in gusts,
he pressed his palms into the raw tips
of her breasts, both worn and heavy,
drooping, pooling in his hands.

He took it, took, and she gave,
resurrected her drawn cleft, her womb
a champion of duty, gorged feracity in bloom.
And when she coughed and wilted, still
he milked her pale bones dry
until the hacking wracked her

and he turned, repulsed, and let her go.

II
One may speak of her fecundity
pressed sodden into dirt
in Tennessee; how her veins now
extend like roots, a complex branching
lined with sighs and parting thoughts,
her scent and dresses, angled cheekbones;
with instructions for the babes
she wouldn't nurse now that her blood
was coughed up, drained; now that she lay back,
eyes sunk, soft, into the earth

III
One wonders, lying naked,
flesh from throttled flesh descended,
what becomes of such breasts, busy,
milked and raw, globed feeding tubes
for mouths that bunch up into cries;
those blushing pillows
into which her children nuzzled, craning
underneath her arms,
brushing their faces on her, desperate
for her lips, her eyes, her skin
Or what becomes of such breasts, heavy,
leaking unseen into evening
with the dirt about her arms
inching and craning in, or fingering
the edges of her dress, its buttons
cracking in the damp; the earth
like lashes on her cheeks, the earth
a mouth over each nipple, pressing
soft, unhurried, clinging
to her hair, her eyes, her skin

Revelation

"Behold, I stand at the door, and knock"
(Revelation 3:20)

Blessed is the man
who keeps the door closed

Ash and Leonard Cohen

Things are very much, for a time,
in their own safekeeping. Consider us, for example,
circling the neighborhood fireworks.

Yet there are silences

in every accent. Something copied, never
pasted – and so, lost. Unintentional suppression
at the Seam of Things. Not unlike two lips --

I've left a lot unexplained.

But then there's this: with every human,
we see further into the painting. Back behind,
eventually, is ash. And Leonard Cohen.

An expert pair of stars.

But always out there, as if God had spoken,
Out with the beautiful; in
with one aim to substitute

diabolical abstractions for concrete persons.

Here's a good example:
How I've been throwing cinder blocks,
assorted rocks at the world, and yet

I am a loop,

a self-made backlash on the low plane
of deepening roots. I've seen all of us
studying, listening to public spaces,

waiting to bewitch each other,

every human being scratched up, fucked.
Not one of us can resist the noble aspects
of a circle. *What about the possibility*

of finding its unbroken, marvelous curve?

And so, the rocks. It's a version of loving,
where every sentence ends with the words
"War or Naked Limbs." The only recourse
is to name one's self, and hold the margins

wide enough to walk in.

Meanwhile, darling, consider my ears
plastered against your disappointment. Out
with the beautiful; come on, out. Someday
I'll buy your silences wholesale.

I'll fill my hands with ash.

the Old Silence

where

    blackness sits

        You draw nearer and break that mass which is my   heart

See how it is torn, its fragments   setting your heavens alight

O my dear God!

Those

    villainous, biting, wire-embraces
   sealed in me more strange forms and faces
Than children see in dreams

For As Wide As This Table Is

there's not enough room
for our two plates and cups,
for our silver, wine, our tongues
useless, hot in our two mouths,
hidden taut behind our napkins,
sputtering

some misery or chore, a laugh,
a quiet infestation, until
our skins, inflating, dough-like,
swallow touches, glances, air;
we have to breathe in slivers slid
between our folds of flesh.

Dinner cooling, tasteless, we etch
lines into the wood to feel
it singe beneath our nails; a plate
moves centimeters, grinding;
the food is gray and silent; we pick
at it like a scab.

Years ago you danced like Swayze
in your jeans, I laughed and pulled up
on my skirt—the table moving
underneath us like a planet.
I say grace now, and blushing, can't
get far enough away; that planet

shrunken into wood and our eight limbs
holding their breaths, as if
they'll knock and flail or splinter

with the slightest birdlike sigh.
I push my chair back, stand, and here
you're close enough to kiss; I feel

my mouth burning with sound – I clear
my throat and hover, pale.
There's soapy water in the sink,
I take our plates and walk them in,
imagining I hold them under
water til they're still.

The Zero

In the beginning was the zero.
And the zero was naught and spoke naught,
was with naught, flamed not into light.
The zero built naught, begat naught,
it ruled naught, rejoiced not,
it drove not the dark from the deep.
The zero knew naught and formed naught,
had seen naught and loved naught,
it hovered not over the waters.
It felt not its right from its left.
It cursed naught and vowed naught,
was over naught, under naught,
in naught and drew not its breath.
The zero heard naught and sang naught,
it wept not, forgave naught;
it rested not after six days.

The zero was in the beginning.
The zero was naught and was with naught.
The zero flamed not into light.

(For Our Struggle Is Not Against Flesh and Blood)

If you had feet, we would lurch up
from the earth, buck against your grey
arches, make fires there
to char your flaking skin—just to smell
some solid transformation,
some divine emanation
But you don't have feet

If you had arms, we would rend you
east to west, snap one rib from the next,
would discard those empty limbs
ever too short, ever too cold,
that never embraced a sparrow
(much less a human soul)
But you don't have arms

If you had a mouth, we would force words
from it, tie you up sweaty—
leering, *Say it!*
and maybe you would. But either way
we'd cut out your tongue, a souvenir, indulgence,
saying, *Watch us speak with the tongues of angels!*
But you don't have a mouth

If you had balls, we would flail at them, sobbing,
would gather the blunt force of centuries
to bludgeon your sacred sac --
A recompense for silence,
for bravado, for that reverberating
IMP   O   TENCE
But you don't have balls

If you had a heart, we would press our ears
to your cold hide; quiet to hear a beat, a thrum,
and maybe we would. But either way
we'd cut you open, drain you dry
to drink that blood, bathe in it, see if there's any
power in it—that ancient wine
But you don't have a heart

When We Left the Homestead

The land rose up behind us:
a swath of brown and metal, cloud;
bisected by the rumbling of a train.

Looking back, we saw the ancient
rooftop, small, out on the field—
curving and rusted like a spoon.

Below it, the old kitchen floor
was swept and every edge
of every countertop was chipping.

A loaf of bread sat wrapped up, still
in plastic in a corner. In the far room:
just a bed frame, one leg broken, and a book.

And back behind the house was Corrie,
hair done and her best dress on,
her fingers curled and feet splayed.

Corrie, such a good girl. When we left her
she was solemn; she lay quiet, with her mouth
drawn open, yawning underground.

Moments Before

Was that really you
with your hand raised
in that picture like a fool
saluting the savage south wall
(greyed out, a thin blurred line
dividing you—your carpet,
bookcase, sweater, glass –
from the wide world at its back)?
Did you really look upon it,
reckless, coy, believing it would hold,
would dissuade a slap
against the face of any knowns
as it rushed in, up, too near,
and with it, coughs of dust
and death from galaxies of stars?
(that the latter coated windows
but could never brush your tongue?)
Did you really never see the man,
his camera on your face, or me,
behind it, young, suspicious, saying
I don't know, don't know—

I Loved Someone Once

He pulled it out in grunts,
a bloody birth,

discarded it in steel trays,
his gloved hands suturing me
shut, barren; as if to say,

No one else shall be
where my rod, my staff
have been

I Knew It Would Be Thus
"thy goodness is as a morning cloud, and as the early dew it goeth away." (Hosea vi 4)

   my God!

   thou didst lie before

I should have checked thy madness

       killed
That seed, which thou
In me didst sow

He Said He Was Dostoevsky.

He wrote with his left fingers
gripping the edge of his chair, his pants
so short his ankles shone bone-bare
above the floor. His back sweating.
Somewhere near his mastoid bone a string
loosened, quivered, its tremor seeping deep
into his skull. He saw the fronts
and backs of continents, the undersides
of ships. He said, this is the dressing gown,
the underground, the cab. And this the whore,
the tea and biscuits. The stain on the left knee,
the scrawled remembered life we want to peel
off like a skin. The wet snow.
He let the words burn through his pen like fire
ants, like needles. Sometimes he laughed
and when he did, he paled, and chewed his tongue.
He left it unredeemed – his hero like a sore.
And then he slept, the string still
shuddering, the universe a lap
into which his crumbs were falling, or a curl
against his spine, now a soaking collar,
now a girl on the front steps.

Morphine

They said,

"Darling, pull the dark on like a sheen
And ask God (or whoever) to dream
in sterilized silver and pale."

They paraded like glass on a string
They went down like homemade ice cream
and God (with a chuckle) said, "Note to self, dear."

Thus we dangled like twin figurines
with God (like a lover) between
and warmed ourselves by our own hot bones.

It was a quarter past everything
when God (with a swagger) was seen
looking grey and acutely serene

Like the world was a stir of his spoon.

Worm

*"If even the moon does not shine,
And the stars are not pure in His sight,
How much less man, who is a maggot,
And a son of man, who is a worm?" (Job 25:5-6)*

Ah, I believed it;
groaned and waited,
knelt and hated
passion, skin,
my breasts and limbs,
my lungs too small and weak
to breathe the thin air at your feet,
which were wriggling, incomplete,
all bruised and swollen.

I learned your verses, hymns
until they mildewed,
blurred, grew brittle, thin;
until I wept for what we both knew
wasn't coming in the end:
your horse and choir, earth agape
and heaven rushing in.

So I covered me in ashes, rolled
the centuries behind me, swallowed
lust and songs like sugar,
packed the meat on, sold my soul.
There were ghosts of you in dresses,
books, and lampshades; every cold
unbuttoned bastard bore your name:
undressed himself, mining for gold.

You're still here in the dust, disease,
the wish to peel the skin from me,
to wash me down to bones and teeth
if doing so could make me clean.
I still trust nothing less than me;
what's left of you is just that keen
and yet-unmatched facility
with which you search a soul and see

a worm.

Things We Don't Know

Who his father was. And where
in the mountains his siblings ran,
and when they cut him off.
When her legs first opened to him
under threat of loneliness or cold.
His brand of cigarettes.
Whether he could read.
The smell of his shirt at dinnertime.
The shape of his hat.
When he first knew he wouldn't keep his pants up
though his children were heaped in the kitchen.
Whether his words were gentle.
His gait in the morning; his gait in the evening.
When he first tasted liquor.
Whether he taught the boys to fish.
Whether he knew their names.
Where his God had gone.
If he knew he was about to die.
If he was relieved.
The songs he sang when he drank.
The length of his daughters' skirts.
His hand on a lover's back.
His way with a horse, an axe, a plate of eggs.
The edge of his smile.
The pain in his side, the doubling over.
The number of times he circled the house
before entering.

Moses Prepares A Eulogy

Moses peeled the sea back, laid it bare:
the dry earth with its heaves and valleys low,
just like you pull this thread into the light

and tie it like a ribbon in your hair.
You bind the arms and ankles of your soul,
then peel its thick skin back to lay it bare.

You'd know that blood, that tissue anywhere!
The color in your cheeks now rises, slow,
you're still pulling the thread into the light.

Moses squints, leans forward in his chair
and asks which trembling self you think you know:
the you that peels this skin back, laying bare

your soul, or your hacked soul itself? Aware
that Moses isn't one to let things go,
you pull the thread still further toward the light

and hand it to him. Moses grins, prepares
a speech for that blank moment when you'll grope
against the peeling-back, the laying-bare.
He pulls the thread—full, frayed—into the light.

Should This Reach You Feeling Rejected and Forlorn

When you came, we'd cleared our plates
and gone to bed. You merely caught us
by surprise. So sorry
not to have expected you!
We would have saved you
something, strung up lights,
put away our things. But we can't change
that now. And anyway, you knew
you weren't the miracle
we'd hoped for. Just a fold and crease
in patterns set upon us at our births.
We held our arms out
and you slid into us, bursting in our veins.
But when we woke, we were the same.

Dear, don't be discouraged.
If you come again, bring something stronger.
Call, and we'll wait up.

How the Secret Got Out

What got hidden in the bedroom
(never shuddered into words)
found its way into her body.

The silence was linguistic:
was of integration, letters,
of a conscious, clean narration.

But we heard It, loud
and flailing, in the shrinking
from hellos, in that invulnerable

poise, and in the face she wore –
that caricature of levity
we feared

and in the thick and sleepy quiet
of those mornings, all the lights off,
when she held her head against it—

tried to keep from throwing up.
It spoke up in her organs,
and again in blood and fascia,

bone, in skin and throat,
in swelling joints to mock the tongue:
no physiological antecedent.

We saw those Non-Words skin her
from the inside, watched them leave her
sick and silent in the swaddling

of an aging, speechless flesh.

Palm Sunday
*"What good is it for a man to gain the whole world,
yet forfeit his soul?" (Mark 8:36)*

This is our forfeiture:
This ear against the latticework,
this breath against the cheek,
these knees locked at the altar.
A palm leaf waving meekly
in the breeze. An empty street.

Bush

*"I will read thy book, and never move
Till I have found therein thy love" (George Herbert)*

You were the flesh, the words,
stamped into a feast
of ink and milk-white brick.
I ate and drank; my soul
in fever lurching in,

but at a ghost, a *ghost*! O god,
that hunger was like glass
in my blood, scraping
at the insides of my veins;

it burned and yawned,
a hot wide well—though drenched—
in flames,
and I, the bush
that would not be consumed

Once You Had Hands

like a mother's.
That was a long time ago.
Since then, I've woken
in the middle of the Psalms
sweating, scared you heard
the prayer I uttered in my sleep
(unwilling), that you'd answer
and it'd feel just like it used to –
like a hot drink down the throat,
like being swaddled, wrung –
and that I wouldn't tell you *no*. Afraid
you'd move and I would too, a tidal pull
I can't resist, temptation massive
as a moon. I don't know when
the dreaming started, why I rush
into the Babylons, Bathshebas,
why I turn your oaths on spits
to watch them burn. I don't know why
none of the kings' horses and men
could ever make you come, deliver,
why they offered you their bodies, wine,
and still you wouldn't eat. I only know
how I keep dreaming, asking,
How long, Lord? and how the blood
drains from my lips, how in my sleep
I soak my pillow, shirt, and wake
with one hand firm against my brow.
It isn't yours.

I hug a strong despair,
and give these hopes a grave

                    I retreat
Unto that hour
Which showed thee last

I search, and rack my soul to see
Those beams again,
But nothing

These errors grieve: and now I must forget
Those pleased ideas I did frame and set
Unto my self

I made sacred these fancies

This silent courtship

But I am now awaked; forgive my dream

And pardon   that I so long have had
Such good thoughts of you, I am not so mad
As to continue them

INDEX OF PHOTOGRAPHS

Cornfield, Indiana, 2008   **Cover Photo**
Evening Porch, Youngstown, Ohio, 2000   **4**
Cheesecloth, Cincinnati, Ohio, 2012   **10**
Newspaper Wallpaper, Colorado, 1997   **19**
Kudzu Figure, Georgia, 1999   **24**
Smoke, North Carolina, 2003   **29**
Carnival, Indiana, 1998   **38**
Dust and Mop, Seymour, Indiana, 2009   **43**
Hotel Laundry, Burbank, California, 2002   **49**
Shadow in Stairwell, Cincinnati, Ohio, 2004   **52**
Blinds and Smoke, North Carolina, 2003   **58**
Lower Ninth, New Orleans, Louisiana, 2010   **66**
February Hands, Cincinnati, Ohio, 1999   **74**
Abandoned Farm, Iowa, 2008   **82**

ABOUT THE AUTHOR

Tasha Golden is the frontwoman and songwriter for the critically-acclaimed band Ellery (ellerymusic.com). Her songs have been heard in major motion pictures, TV dramas, radio, and more. Her poetry and prose have been published in *Pleaides*, *Ethos Journal*, and *Coldnoon Poetics*, among others. She researches the impact of the arts on social silences, and blogs for *Ploughshares* literary journal.

www.tashagolden.com

www.ingramcontent.com/pod-product-compliance
Lightning Source LLC
Chambersburg PA
CBHW070132100426
42744CB00009B/1812

www.ingramcontent.com/pod-product-compliance
Lightning Source LLC
Chambersburg PA
CBHW061603110426
42742CB00039B/2737